Das Buch

»Technik, wie ich sie ‹ ausschließlich des Dichters habung von Metrum, Rl sie meint auch eine Del ... ...ung dem Leben gegenüber, eine Definition seiner eigenen Wirklichkeit. Sie meint das Aufspüren von Wegen hinaus aus seinen normalen kognitiven Bindungen durch einen Sturm auf das Ungesagte ...« Das dichterische Werk des Iren Seamus Heaney gehört in der anglo-amerikanischen Welt zu den herausragenden Leistungen der modernen Poesie.

Der Autor

Seamus Justin Heaney wurde am 13. April 1939 in Castledawson (Nordirland) geboren, studierte und lehrte an der Universität Belfast und übersiedelte 1972 in die Republik Irland. Nach vielen internationalen Ehrungen wurde er im Juni 1989 zum »poeta laureatus« der Universität Oxford gewählt und erhielt 1995 den Nobelpreis für Literatur. Werke: ›Death of a naturalist‹ (1966), ›Door into the dark‹ (1969), ›Wintering out‹ (1972), ›North‹ (1975), ›Field work‹ (1979), ›Preoccupations‹ (1980), ›Selected Poems 1965–75‹ (1980), ›Station Island‹ (1984), ›The Haw Lantern‹ (1987), Gedichte.

Seamus Heaney
Die Hagebuttenlaterne
The Haw Lantern

Aus dem Englischen von
Giovanni Bandini und Ditte König

Deutscher
Taschenbuch
Verlag

dtv

Die Originalausgabe erschien unter dem Titel
›The Haw Lantern‹
bei Faber & Faber Ltd., London 1987

Ungekürzte Ausgabe
November 1995
2. Auflage Dezember 1995
Deutscher Taschenbuch Verlag GmbH & Co. KG,
München
© 1987 Seamus Heaney
© dieser Ausgabe: Carl Hanser Verlag München Wien 1990
Umschlagentwurf: Dieter Brumshagen
Umschlagfoto: Marianne Fleitmann, Berlin
Gesamtherstellung: Pustet, Regensburg
Printed in Germany · ISBN 3-423-12228-5

Die Hagebuttenlaterne
The Haw Lantern

Für Bernard und Jane McCabe

Das Flußbett – trocken, halb mit Laub gefüllt.
Uns – rauscht ein Fluß, der in den Bäumen schwillt.

The riverbed, dried-up, half-full of leaves.
Us, listening to a river in the trees.

Alphabets

I

A shadow his father makes with joined hands
And thumbs and fingers nibbles on the wall
Like a rabbit's head. He understands
He will understand more when he goes to school.

There he draws smoke with chalk the whole first week,
Then draws the forked stick that they call a Y.
This is writing. A swan's neck and swan's back
Make the 2 he can see now as well as say.

Two rafters and a cross-tie on the slate
Are the letter some call *ah*, some call *ay*.
There are charts, there are headlines, there is a right
Way to hold the pen and a wrong way.

First it is ›copying out‹, and then ›English‹
Marked correct with a little leaning hoe.
Smells of inkwells rise in the classroom hush.
A globe in the window tilts like a coloured O.

II

Declensions sang on air like a *hosanna*
As, column after stratified column,
Book One of *Elementa Latina*,
Marbled and minatory, rose up in him

For he was fostered next in a stricter school
Named for the patron saint of the oak wood
Where classes switched to the pealing of a bell
And he left the Latin forum for the shade

Alphabete

I

Ein Schatten, den sein Vater (mit Händepaar,
Daumen und Fingern) macht, mümmelt an der Wand
Wie ein Häschenkopf. Soviel ist klar:
Mehr wird ihm klar dann in der Schule sein.

Dort malt er Kringelrauch die erste Woche lang,
Malt dann den Stock mit Querstück namens T.
Das ist Schreiben. Hals-und-Buckel eines Schwans
Machen die 2 sichtbar: Sie *sagen* kann er eh.

Zwei Sparren und ein Balken auf der Tafel
Sind der Buchstabe *ah* (so seine Lautgestaltung).
Es gibt Karten, Überschriften, eine richtige Griffel-
haltung gibt's und eine falsche Haltung.

»Schreiben« ist es zuerst, und später »Englisch«;
Lehnt eine kleine Hacke dran, heißt's: richtig so!
Tintengeruch steigt in der Klassenzimmerstille.
Ein Globus am Fenster kippt wie ein buntes O.

II

Flexionen hallten luftig wie ein *Hosanna*,
Während, Turm um Schichtenturm von Formen,
Band Eins von *Elementa Latina*,
Mahnend und marmoriert, in ihm emporwuchs.

Denn er bezog dann eine strengere Schule,
Benannt nach dem Patron des Eichenwaldes,
In der die Stunden nach dem Schlag der Glocke spulten
Und er, nach dem *forum* des Lateins, den Schatten

Of new calligraphy that felt like home.
The letters of this alphabet were trees.
The capitals were orchards in full bloom,
The lines of script like briars coiled in ditches.

Here in her snooded garment and bare feet,
All ringleted in assonance and woodnotes,
The poet's dream stole over him like sunlight
And passed into the tenebrous thickets.

He learns this other writing. He is the scribe
Who drove a team of quills on his white field.
Round his cell door the blackbirds dart and dab.
Then self-denial, fasting, the pure cold.

By rules that hardened the farther they reached north
He bends to his desk and begins again.
Christ's sickle has been in the undergrowth.
The script grows bare and Merovingian.

III

The globe has spun. He stands in a wooden O.
He alludes to Shakespeare. He alludes to Graves.
Time has bulldozed the school and school window.
Balers drop bales like printouts where stooked sheaves

Made lambdas on the stubble once at harvest
And the delta face of each potato pit
Was patted straight and moulded against frost.
All gone, with the omega that kept

Watch above each door, the good luck horse-shoe.
Yet shape-note language, absolute on air
As Constantine's sky-lettered IN HOC SIGNO
Can still command him; or the necromancer

Neuer Kalligraphie wie Heimat fühlte.
Die Zeichen dieses Alphabets waren Bäume.
Die Großbuchstaben Obstgärten in voller Blüte,
Die Zeilen Gräben, wirr von Dornensträuchern.

Bebänderten Gewands und barfuß stahl sich,
Ringelgelockt von Assonanz und Singen,
Des Dichters Traum hier über ihn wie Sonnenlicht,
Um dann in düstrem Dickicht zu versinken.

Er lernt diese andere Schrift. Er ist der Schreiber,
Der ein Kielgespann trieb über sein weißes Feld.
Vor seiner Zelle picken Amseln, flattern.
Dann Selbstverleugnung, Fasten, reine Kälte.

Nach Regeln, starrer, je nördlicher sie kamen,
Beugt er sich, neu beginnend, über seinen Tisch.
Die Sichel Christi ist durchs Unterholz gefahren.
Die Schrift wird karg und merowingisch.

III

Der Globus drehte sich. Er steht in einem O aus Holz.
Er spielt auf Shakespeare an. Auf Robert Graves.
Die Zeit hat Schule und Fenster eingewalzt.
Mähdrescher stanzen Ballen, wo gedockte Garben

Zur Ernte Lambdas auf den Stoppeln machten,
Und man den Delta-Kopf jeder Kartoffelmiete
Festknetete und -klopfte gegen Frost.
Vergangen auch das Omega; es hielt

Wache über jeder Tür, das Glückshufeisen.
Doch kann das Bild-Wort, absolut im Äther
Wie Konstantins HOC SIGNO-Himmelszeichen,
Ihm noch was sagen; oder dem Beschwörer,

Who would hang from the domed ceiling of his house
A figure of the world with colours in it
So that the figure of the universe
And ›not just single things‹ would meet his sight

When he walked abroad. As from his small window
The astronaut sees all he has sprung from,
The risen, aqueous, singular, lucent O
Like a magnified and buoyant ovum –

Or like my own wide pre-reflective stare
All agog at the plasterer on his ladder
Skimming our gable and writing our name there
With his trowel point, letter by strange letter.

Der an die Deckenwölbung seines Hauses
Ein Bildnis von der Welt mit ihren Farben
Zu hängen pflegte, daß das Bild des Kosmos
Und »nicht bloß Einzeldinge« seine Augen träfen,

Wenn er spazierenging. Der Astronaut sieht so
Aus seinem kleinen Fenster alles, was ihm Leben
Gab: das aufgegangene, feuchte, eine, klare O,
Wie ein Ovum, ausgedehnt und schwebend –

Oder wie mein staunend vorbewußtes Starren
Auf den Verputzer, der auf seiner Bühne
Unseren Giebel glättet und darauf unseren Namen
Mit der Spitze der Kelle schreibt, Rune um Rune.

Terminus

I

When I hoked there, I would find
An acorn and a rusted bolt.

If I lifted my eyes, a factory chimney
And a dormant mountain.

If I listened, an engine shunting
And a trotting horse.

Is it any wonder when I thought
I would have second thoughts?

II

When they spoke of the prudent squirrel's hoard
It shone like gifts at a nativity.

When they spoke of the mammon of iniquity
The coins in my pockets reddened like stove-lids.

I was the march drain and the march drain's banks
Suffering the limit of each claim.

Grenzstation

I

Wenn ich mich bückte, fand ich dort
Eine Eichel und einen rostigen Bolzen.

Hob ich die Augen, einen Fabrikschlot
Und einen ruhenden Berg.

Hörte ich hin, eine Rangierlok
Und ein trabendes Pferd.

Ist es denn ein Wunder, wenn ich dachte,
Ich dächte allem nach?

II

Sprachen sie vom Hort des klugen Hörnchens,
Glänzte er wie Gaben zur Geburt des Kindes.

Sprachen sie vom schnöden Unrechts-Mammon,
Erglühten meine Groschen rot wie Öfen.

Ich war der Grenz-Siel und die Grenzsiel-Ufer,
Das Ausmaß jeder Forderung erleidend.

III

Two buckets were easier carried than one.
I grew up in between.

My left hand placed the standard iron weight.
My right tilted a last grain in the balance.

Baronies, parishes met where I was born.
When I stood on the central stepping stone

I was the last earl on horseback in midstream
Still parleying, in earshot of his peers.

III

Zwei Bündel trugen sich leichter als eins.
Ich wuchs dazwischen auf.

Meine Linke plazierte das eiserne Gewicht.
Die Rechte gab ein letztes Korn zum Ausgleich.

Baronien, Sprengel trafen sich, wo ich zur Welt kam.
Stand ich auf dem Trittstein in der Mitte,

War ich der letzte Graf, zu Roß auf halber Furt,
Noch unterhandelnd, in Hörweite seiner Herren.

From the Frontier of Writing

The tightness and the nilness round that space
when the car stops in the road, the troops inspect
its make and number and, as one bends his face

towards your window, you catch sight of more
on a hill beyond, eyeing with intent
down cradled guns that hold you under cover

and everything is pure interrogation
until a rifle motions and you move
with guarded unconcerned acceleration –

a little emptier, a little spent
as always by that quiver in the self,
subjugated, yes, and obedient.

So you drive on to the frontier of writing
where it happens again. The guns on tripods;
the sergeant with his on-off mike repeating

data about you, waiting for the squawk
of clearance; the marksman training down
out of the sun upon you like a hawk.

And suddenly you're through, arraigned yet freed,
as if you'd passed from behind a waterfall
on the black current of a tarmac road

past armour-plated vehicles, out between
the posted soldiers flowing and receding
like tree shadows into the polished windscreen.

Von der Grenze des Schreibens

Die Enge um diesen Raumabschnitt, das Nichts,
als das Auto anhält, die Soldaten Marke
und Nummer überprüfen und du, als einer sein Gesicht

zu deinem Fenster beugt, dahinter weitere siehst,
auf einem Hügel, die mit klarem Vorsatz
entlang des Laufs dich deckender MPis

zu dir herabschauen, und alles schier Verhör ist,
bis ein Gewehr »na los« nickt und du, sorgsam
unbeteiligt beschleunigend, davonfährst –

ein bißchen leerer und ein bißchen lahm,
wie stets von diesem Zittern in der Seele,
übermannt, ja untertänig zahm.

So fährst du weiter bis zur Grenze des Schreibens,
wo es nochmal geschieht. Die MGs auf Ständern;
der Sergeant mit dem Mikro, deine Personalien

repetierend und aufs Krächzen, das dich freispricht,
wartend; der Scharfschütze, von der Sonne aus
dich kühl ins Auge fassend wie ein Habicht.

Und plötzlich bist du durch, angeklagt doch frei-
gesetzt, gleichsam durch einen Wasserfall
auf einen schwarzen Asphalt-Strom gelangt, vorbei

an Panzerspähwagen, ins Freie, zwischen
den Posten, die wie Baum-Schatten zurückweichen
und in die blanke Windschutzscheibe huschen.

The Haw Lantern

The wintry haw is burning out of season,
crab of the thorn, a small light for small people,
wanting no more from them but that they keep
the wick of self-respect from dying out,
not having to blind them with illumination.

But sometimes when your breath plumes in the frost
it takes the roaming shape of Diogenes
with his lantern, seeking one just man;
so you end up scrutinized from behind the haw
he holds up at eye-level on its twig,
and you flinch before its bonded pith and stone,
its blood-prick that you wish would test and clear you,
its pecked-at ripeness that scans you, then moves on.

Die Hagebuttenlaterne

Die winterharte Frucht erglüht zur Unzeit,
Apfel des Dorns, ein kleines Licht für kleine Leute,
das nur von ihnen will, daß sie den Docht
der Selbstachtung am Leben halten,
und es nicht nötig hat, mit Glanz zu blenden.

Doch manchmal, wenn dein Atem frostig pludert,
wird er zur schweifenden Gestalt Diogenes'
mit der Laterne, der nach seinem Mann sucht;
so spürst du auf einmal hinter dieser Frucht,
die er in Augenhöhe hält, den Schätzblick
und schreckst zurück vor ihrem dürren Fleisch,
vor ihrem Stich (daß er dich prüfte und freigäb!),
ihrer angepickten Reife, die dich mißt, dann weiterzieht.

The Stone Grinder

Penelope worked with some guarantee of a plot.
Whatever she unweaved at night
might advance it all by a day.

Me, I ground the same stones for fifty years
and what I undid was never the thing I had done.
I was unrewarded as darkness at a mirror.

I prepared my surface to survive what came over it –
cartographers, printmakers, all that lining and inking.
I ordained opacities and they haruspicated.

For them it was a new start and a clean slate
every time. For me, it was coming full circle
like the ripple perfected in stillness.

So. To commemorate me. Imagine the faces
stripped off the face of a quarry. Practise
coitus interruptus on a pile of old lithographs.

Der Steinschleifer

Penelopes Arbeit entbehrt' nicht der Methode.
Was immer sie des Nachts auftrennte,
rückte das Ganze um einen Tag nach vorn.

Ich schleif denselben Stein seit fünfzig Jahren,
und was ich verdarb, war niemals mein eigenes Werk.
Ich blieb unbelohnt wie Dunkelheit vorm Spiegel.

Ich hab mein Äußeres aufs Überdauern vorbereitet –
Karto- und Lithographen, all das Gestrichel und Getinte.
Ich verfügte Undurchsichtigkeit, und sie haruspizierten.

Für sie war es ein Neubeginn, Tabula rasa,
jedesmal. Für mich ein sich schließender Kreislauf,
wie die Ring-Welle, in Stillstand vollendet.

So. Mir zum Gedächtnis. Stell dir die Fratzen vor,
von der Front eines Steinbruchs geschält. Übe
Coitus interruptus auf einem Stapel alter Lithos.

A Daylight Art

for Norman MacCaig

On the day he was to take the poison
Socrates told his friends he had been writing:
putting Aesop's fables into verse.

And this was not because Socrates loved wisdom
and advocated the examined life.
The reason was that he had had a dream.

Caesar, now, or Herod or Constantine
or any number of Shakespearean kings
bursting at the end like dams

where original panoramas lie submerged
which have to rise again before the death scenes –
you can believe in their believing dreams.

But hardly Socrates. Until, that is,
he tells his friends the dream had kept recurring
all his life, repeating one instruction:

Practise the art, which art until that moment
he always took to mean philosophy.
Happy the man, therefore, with a natural gift

for practising the right one from the start –
poetry, say, or fishing; whose nights are dreamless;
whose deep-sunk panoramas rise and pass

like daylight through the rod's eye or the nib's eye.

Eine Tageslicht-Kunst

für Norman MacCaig

Am Tag, als er den Schierling trinken sollte,
erzählte Sokrates den Freunden, er habe geschrieben:
die Fabeln des Äsop versifiziert.

Der Grund war nicht, daß er die Weisheit liebte
und für das reflektierte Leben eintrat.
Er hatte vielmehr einen Traum gehabt.

Nun, Cäsar, Herodes oder Konstantin
und soviel Shakespeare-Könige du willst,
(berstend gegen Ende wie ein Staudamm,

wo frühere Aussichten versunken liegen
und wieder hoch müssen, vor der Sterbeszene) –
daß *die* an Träume glaubten, ist schon glaubhaft.

Doch schwerlich Sokrates. Zumindest, bis
er seinen Freunden sagt, der Traum habe sich ständig,
sein Leben lang, mit *einer* Weisung wiederholt:

Übe die Kunst – worunter er bis dahin
stets die Philosophie verstanden habe.
Glücklich also der Mann mit der Begabung,

von Anfang an die richtige zu üben –
Dichtung etwa, oder Fischerei; dessen Nächte traumlos sind;
dessen versunkene Bilder steigen und vorübergehen

wie Tageslicht am Gnomon der Angel oder des Stifts.

Parable Island

I

Although they are an occupied nation
and their only border is an inland one
they yield to nobody in their belief
that the country is an island.

Somewhere in the far north, in a region
every native thinks of as ›the coast‹,
there lies the mountain of the shifting names.

The occupiers call it Cape Basalt.
The Sun's Headstone, say farmers in the east.
Drunken westerners call it The Orphan's Tit.

To find out where he stands the traveller
has to keep listening – since there is no map
which draws the line he knows he must have crossed.

Meanwhile, the forked-tongued natives keep repeating
prophecies they pretend not to believe
about a point where all the names converge
underneath the mountain and where (some day)
they are going to start to mine the ore of truth.

II

In the beginning there was one bell-tower
which struck its single note each day at noon
in honour of the one-eyed all-creator.

Parabolische Insel

I

Obwohl sie eine besetzte Nation sind
und ihre einzige Grenze ganz im Inland liegt,
bringt sie kein Mensch von ihrem Glauben ab,
das Land sei eine Insel.

Hoch im Norden irgendwo, in einer Gegend,
die jeder Einheimische als »die Küste« kennt,
da liegt der Berg der wechselhaften Namen.

Die Besatzer nennen ihn Cape Basalt.
Der Sonnengrabstein, sagen Bauern im Osten.
Betrunkene Westler nennen ihn Die Waisenpiez'.

Der Reisende, der seinen Standpunkt sucht,
muß weiter lauschen – da ihm keine Karte
die Grenze weist, die er wohl überschritt.

Inzwischen wiederholen die Landeskinder
spaltzüngig »ungeglaubte« Prophetien
von einem Punkt, wo sich alle Namen treffen
– unter dem Berg – und wo sie (einst) beginnen
werden, das Erz der Wahrheit abzubauen.

II

Im Anfang gab es einen Glockenturm,
der täglich seinen einen Ton zu Mittag schlug
zu Ehren des einäugigen Allschöpfers.

At least, this was the original idea
missionary scribes record they found
in autochthonous tradition. But even there

you can't be sure that parable is not
at work already retrospectively,
since all their early manuscripts are full

of stylized eye-shapes and recurrent glosses
in which those old revisionists derive
the word *island* from roots in *eye* and *land*.

III

Now archaeologists begin to gloss the glosses.
To one school, the stone circles are pure symbol;
to another, assembly spots or hut foundations.

One school thinks a post-hole in an ancient floor
stands first of all for a pupil in an iris.
The other thinks a post-hole is a post-hole. And so on –

like the subversives and collaborators
always vying with a fierce possessiveness
for the right to set ›the island story‹ straight.

IV

The elders dream of boat-journeys and havens
and have their stories too, like the one about the man
who took to his bed, it seems, and died convinced

that the cutting of the Panama Canal
would mean the ocean would all drain away
and the island disappear by aggrandizement.

Zum mindesten war dies die Ur-Vorstellung,
welche die Mönche, laut Missionsbericht,
für autochthon befanden. Doch selbst da

kann man nicht sicher sein, ob die Parabel
nicht schon retrospektiv am Wirken sei,
da ihre frühen Manuskripte sämtlich

voll stilisierter Augen sind und Glossen,
in denen diese Alt-Revisionisten
Irland aus *Land* und *Iris* derivieren.

III

Die Archäologen glossieren jetzt die Glossen.
Den einen sind die Steinkreise rein symbolisch;
den anderen Versammlungsplätze, Hüttenmauern.

Eine Schule meint, ein Pfahlloch in antikem Pflaster
bedeute erst einmal eine Pupille.
Die andere meint, ein Pfahlloch sei ein Pfahlloch. Und so weiter –

wie die Rebellen und Kollaborateure
ständig streitend um das alleinige Recht,
die »Insel-Geschichte« Korrektur zu lesen.

IV

Die Alten träumen von Schiffsreisen und Häfen
und haben auch Geschichten – so wie die vom Mann,
der krank wurde und starb, scheint's, überzeugt,

die Eröffnung des Panamakanals
würde bedeuten, daß der ganze Ozean abläuft,
und die Insel durch Vergrößerung verschwindet.

From the Republic of Conscience

I

When I landed in the republic of conscience
it was so noiseless when the engines stopped
I could hear a curlew high above the runway.

At immigration, the clerk was an old man
who produced a wallet from his homespun coat
and showed me a photograph of my grandfather.

The woman in customs asked me to declare
the words of our traditional cures and charms
to heal dumbness and avert the evil eye.

No porters. No interpreter. No taxi.
You carried your own burden and very soon
your symptoms of creeping privilege disappeared.

II

Fog is a dreaded omen there but lightning
spells universal good and parents hang
swaddled infants in trees during thunderstorms.

Salt is their precious mineral. And seashells
are held to the ear during births and funerals.
The base of all inks and pigments is seawater.

Their sacred symbol is a stylized boat.
The sail is an ear, the mast a sloping pen,
The hull a mouth-shape, the keel an open eye.

Aus der Republik des Gewissens

I

Als ich in der Republik des Gewissens landete,
war es so still, als die Motoren stoppten,
daß ich ein Brachhuhn hörte, hoch über der Rollbahn.

Der Paßbeamte war ein alter Mann,
der ein Portefeuille aus seiner Joppe zog
und mir ein Foto meines Ahnen zeigte.

Die Frau am Zoll verlangte meine Erklärung
unserer traditionellen Zaubersprüche,
um Stummheit zu heilen und gegen den bösen Blick.

Keine Träger. Kein Dolmetscher. Kein Taxi.
Du trugst dein Bündel selbst, und schon sehr bald
verschwand jedes Symptom schleichenden Vorrechts.

II

Nebel verheißt dort Schlimmes, doch der Blitz
bedeutet Glück und Heil, und Eltern hängen
Wickelkinder in die Bäume bei Gewitter.

Salz ist ihr Edelstein. Und bei Geburten
und Leichenfeiern lauscht man dem Meer in Schneckenhäusern.
Der Grundstoff jeder Tinte und Farbe ist Meerwasser.

Ihr heiliges Symbol ist ein stilisiertes Boot.
Das Segel ist ein Ohr, der Mastbaum eine Feder,
der Rumpf ein Mund, der Kiel ein offenes Auge.

At their inauguration, public leaders
must swear to uphold unwritten law and weep
to atone for their presumption to hold office –

and to affirm their faith that all life sprang
from salt in tears which the sky-god wept
after he dreamt his solitude was endless.

III

I came back from that frugal republic
with my two arms the one length, the customs woman
having insisted my allowance was myself.

The old man rose and gazed into my face
and said that was official recognition
that I was now a dual citizen.

He therefore desired me when I got home
to consider myself a representative
and to speak on their behalf in my own tongue.

Their embassies, he said, were everywhere
but operated independently
and no ambassador would ever be relieved.

Bei Amtseinführung müssen Volksvertreter
schwören, das ungeschriebene Gesetz zu wahren,
und weinen: zur Sühne ihrer Amtsanmaßung –

und als Bekenntnis ihres Glaubens, daß alles Leben
aus Salz entstand, aus Träumen, die der Himmelsgott
weinte, als ihm träumte, seine Einsamkeit sei endlos.

III

Ich verließ diese karge Republik
von keiner Last bedrückt; die Frau am Zoll
hatte darauf beharrt, mein Freigut sei ich selbst.

Der Alte erhob sich und fixierte mich:
Dies sei die offizielle Anerkennung
meiner jetzt doppelten Nationalität.

Er wünsche daher, daß ich nach meiner Heimkehr
mich als Beauftragten verstehen möge
und für sie das Wort in meiner Sprache ergreife.

Ihre Botschaften, sagte er, seien überall,
arbeiteten jedoch ganz unabhängig,
und kein Botschafter werde jemals abberufen.

Hailstones

I

My cheek was hit and hit:
sudden hailstones
pelted and bounced on the road.

When it cleared again
something whipped and knowledgeable
had withdrawn

and left me there with my chances.
I made a small hard ball
of burning water running from my hand

just as I make this now
out of the melt of the real thing
smarting into its absence.

II

To be reckoned with, all the same,
those brats of showers.
The way they refused permission,

rattling the classroom window
like a ruler across the knuckles,
the way they were perfect first

and then in no time dirty slush.
Thomas Traherne had his orient wheat
for proof and wonder

Hagelkörner

I

Auf meiner Wange Schlag auf Schlag:
plötzlicher Hagel
prasselte und prallte auf die Straße.

Als es wieder aufklarte
hatte sich etwas, ausgepeitscht und kenntnisreich,
zurückgezogen

und mich mit meinen Chancen stehenlassen.
Ich machte einen kleinen harten Ball
brennenden Wassers das mir aus der Hand lief

so wie ich jetzt das
aus der Schmelze des Wirklichen mache
das in sein Fortsein schmerzt.

II

Trotzdem nicht zu unterschätzen,
diese Schauer-Gören.
So, wie sie untersagten,

am Klassenfenster rasselten
wie ein Lineal quer über Fingerknöchel,
so, wie sie zuerst vollkommen waren

und dann im Nu schlüpfriger Schmutz.
Thomas Traherne hatte den ewig goldnen Weizen
als Wunder und Beweis,

but for us, it was the sting of hailstones
and the unstingable hands of Eddie Diamond
foraging in the nettles.

III

Nipple and hive, bite-lumps,
small acorns of the almost pleasurable
intimated and disallowed

when the shower ended
and everything said *wait*.
For what? For forty years

to say there, there you had
the truest foretaste of your aftermath –
in that dilation

when the light opened in silence
and a car with wipers going still
laid perfect tracks in the slush.

doch für uns war es das Brennen des Hagels
und die unbrennbare Hand von Eddie Diamond,
der in den Nesseln wühlte.

III

Nippel und Bläschen, Bißmale,
Kleine Eicheln des fast Erfreulichen,
angedeutet und unerlaubt,

als der Schauer endete,
und alles sagte *wart*.
Worauf? Auf vierzig Jahre später

um da zu sagen, da hattest du
den wahrsten Vorgeschmack deiner Folgezeit –
in dieser Weitung

als das Licht sich lautlos auftat
und ein Auto noch mit Wischern an
vollkommene Spuren durch den Matsch zog.

Two Quick Notes

I

My old hard friend, how you sought
Occasions of justified anger!
Who could buff me like you

Who wanted the soul to ring true
And plain as a galvanized bucket
And would kick it to test it?

Or whack it clean like a carpet.
So of course when you turned on yourself
You were ferocious.

II

Abrupt and thornproofed and lonely.
A raider from the old country
Of night prayer and principled challenge,

Crashing at barriers
You thought ought still to be there,
Overshooting into thin air.

O upright self-wounding prie-dieu
In shattered free fall:
Hail and farewell.

Zwei Briefchen

I

Mein alter harter Freund, wie suchtest du
Gelegenheiten für gerechten Zorn!
Wer konnte mich ledern wie du,

Der du wolltest, die Seele sei lauter
Und echt wie ein rostfreier Eimer,
Und den Abkratz-Test machtest?

Oder den Staub aus ihr prügeltest.
Und, ganz klar, als dein Blick auf dich selbst fiel,
Gab's kein Erbarmen.

II

Schroff, dornabweisend und einsam.
Ein Angreifer aus dem alten Land
Des Nachtgebets und grundsätzlichen Anspruchs,

Gegen Schranken krachend,
Die, dachtest du, noch da sein müßten,
Und übers Ziel hinaus, ins Leere.

O starres selbstquälendes Betpult
In freiem Zerfall:
Heil und lebwohl.

The Stone Verdict

When he stands in the judgment place
With his stick in his hand and the broad hat
Still on his head, maimed by self-doubt
And an old disdain of sweet talk and excuses,
It will be no justice if the sentence is blabbed out.
He will expect more than words in the ultimate court
He relied on through a lifetime's speechlessness.

Let it be like the judgment of Hermes,
God of the stone heap, where the stones were verdicts
Cast solidly at his feet, piling up around him
Until he stood waist deep in the cairn
Of his apotheosis: maybe a gate-pillar
Or a tumbled wallstead where hogweed earths the silence
Somebody will break at last to say, ›Here
His spirit lingers,‹ and will have said too much.

Das Stein-Verdikt

Wenn er am Ort des Gerichtes steht,
Mit dem Stock in der Hand, den breiten Hut
Noch auf dem Kopf, zermürbt von Selbstzweifeln
Und alter Verachtung für Floskel und Ausflucht,
Wird ausgeschwatzter Richtspruch niemals Recht sein.
Er wird mehr als Worte erwarten in der letzten Instanz,
Auf die er sich ein stummes Leben lang verließ.

Sei es also wie das Urteil des Hermes,
Gott des Steinhaufens, wo die Steine Verdikte waren,
Fest ihm zu Füßen geworfen, rings um ihn wachsend,
Bis er hüfttief im Steinhügel stand
Seiner Apotheose: vielleicht ein Torpfeiler
Oder Mauerreste, wo Bärenklau das Schweigen erdet,
Das jemand endlich brechen wird mit: »Hier
Schwebt noch sein Geist.« Und das wird schon zuviel sein.

From the Land of the Unspoken

I have heard of a bar of platinum
Kept by a logical and talkative nation
as their standard of measurement,
the throne room and the burial chamber
of every calculation and prediction.
I could feel at home inside that metal core
slumbering at the very hub of systems.

We are a dispersed people whose history
is a sensation of opaque fidelity.
When or why our exile began
among the speech-ridden, we cannot tell
but solidarity comes flooding up in us
when we hear their legends of infants discovered
floating in coracles towards destiny
or of kings' biers heaved and borne away
on the river's shoulders or out into the sea roads.

When we recognize our own, we fall in step
but do not altogether come up level.
My deepest contact was underground
strap-hanging back to back on a rush-hour train
and in a museum once, I inhaled
vernal assent from a neck and shoulder
pretending to be absorbed in a display
of absolutely silent quernstones.

Aus dem Land des Unausgesprochenen

Ich hörte von einem Stab aus Platin,
den sich ein logisches und wortreiches Volk
als Eichmaß und Standard hält –
der Thronsaal und das Grabgewölbe
jeder Berechnung und jeglicher Prognose.
Mir könnt's in diesem harten Kern gefallen,
schlummernd im ruhenden Drehpunkt der Systeme.

Wir sind ein verstreutes Volk, dessen Geschichte
eine Empfindung unbestimmter Treue ist.
Wann oder warum unser Exil begann
unter den Sprachbeherrschten, können wir nicht sagen,
doch wallt es solidarisch in uns auf,
hören wir ihre Sagen von Findelkindern,
schicksalwärts in Weidenkörben treibend,
oder von Fürstenbahren, auf und davongetragen
auf des Flusses Schultern oder fort in die See-Flut.

Erkennen wir uns wieder, fassen wir Tritt,
erreichen aber nicht ganz eine Höhe.
Am tiefsten fühlte ich mich einst berührt
Zur Stoßzeit Rück- an Rücken in der U-Bahn;
und einmal atmete ich, im Museum,
ein frisches Ja von einem Nacken ein,
vorgeblich tief versunken in Betrachtung
vollkommen stummer Mühlstein-Exponate.

Our unspoken assumptions have the force
of revelation. How else could we know
that whoever is the first of us to seek
assent and votes in a rich democracy
will be the last of us and have killed our language?
Meanwhile, if we miss the sight of a fish
we heard jumping and then see its ripples,
that means one more of us is dying somewhere.

Unsere unausgesprochenen Annahmen
sind absolut. Wie sonst könnten wir wissen,
daß wer von uns zuerst in einer reichen
Demokratie Applaus und Stimmen sucht,
der Letzte von uns sein und unsere Sprache
getötet haben wird? Bis dahin gilt:
Wenn wir den Fisch verpassen, den wir springen
hörten, und danach dessen Ringe sehen,
heißt's, irgendwo stirbt wieder einer von uns.

A Ship of Death

Scyld was still a strong man when his time came
and he crossed over into Our Lord's keeping.
His warrior band did what he bade them
when he laid down the law among the Danes:
they shouldered him out to the sea's flood,
the chief they revered who had long ruled them.
A ring-necked prow rode in the harbour,
clad with ice, its cables tightening.
They stretched their beloved lord in the boat,
laid out amidships by the mast
the great ring-giver. Far-fetched treasures
were piled upon him, and precious gear.
I never heard before of a ship so well furbished
with battle-tackle, bladed weapons
and coats of mail. The treasure was massed
on top of him: it would travel far
on out into the sway of ocean.
They decked his body no less bountifully
with offerings than those first ones did
who cast him away when he was a child
and launched him out alone over the waves.
And they set a gold standard up
high above his head and let him drift
to wind and tide, bewailing him
and mourning their loss. No man can tell,
no wise man in the hall or weathered veteran
knows for certain who salvaged that load.

Beowulf, II., 26-52

Ein Schiff des Todes

Scyld war noch ein starker Mann, als seine Stunde kam
und er hinübersetzte in Unseres Herrn Hut.
Seine Krieger-Schar tat nach seinem Bescheid,
da er das Gesetz gebot unter den Dänen:
Sie trugen ihn hinaus zur See-Flut,
den Hochgeachteten, der sie lange beherrscht hatte.
Ein krummhalsiger Kiel lag vor Anker,
starrend vor Frost, seine Trossen stramm.
Sie brachten den herzlieben Herrn in das Boot,
bahrten ihn mittschiffs beim Mast auf,
den großen Ringe-Vergeuder. Fern gefundenes Gut
türmten sie auf ihn, und teures Gerät.
Nie vernahm ich zuvor von einem Schiff, so schön gerüstet
mit Schlacht-Werkzeug, geschliffenen Waffen
und Kettenhemden. Sie häuften den Hort
auf seinen Rumpf: Weit würde er reisen
dann in die Dünung des Nordmeers.
Sie kleideten den Leib nicht minder glanzvoll
mit Geschenken als ihm die andern gaben,
die ihn aussetzten, als er ein Kind war,
und ihn allein aussandten über die See.
Und sie stellten eine Gold-Standarte auf,
hoch über seinem Haupt, und ließen ihn treiben
nach Wind und Tide und beweinten ihn
und beklagten ihren Verlust. Kein Mann kann sagen,
kein Rater in der Halle noch rüstiger Held
weiß mit Bestimmtheit, wer diese Beute barg.

Beowulf II., 26-52

The Spoonbait

So a new similitude is given us
And we say: The soul may be compared

Unto a spoonbait that a child discovers
Beneath the sliding lid of a pencil case,

Glimpsed once and imagined for a lifetime
Risen and free and spooling out of nowhere –

A shooting star going back up the darkness.
It flees him and it burns him all at once

Like the single drop that Dives implored
Falling and falling into a great gulf.

Then exit, the polished helmet of a hero
Laid out amidships above scudding water.

Exit, alternatively, a toy of light
Reeled through him upstream, snagging on nothing.

Der Blinker

Also wird uns ein neues Bild zuteil,
Und wir sagen: Die Seele ist vergleichbar

Einem Blinker, den ein Kind erspäht
Unter dem Deckel eines Federkastens,

Einmal geschaut und lebenslang vermutet:
Erstanden, frei und unversehens entschwirrend –

Sternschnuppe, die zurück ins Dunkel aufsteigt.
Entflieht ihm und verbrennt ihn unverhofft

Wie der eine Tropfen, den der Reiche erflehte
Und fällt und fällt in eine große Kluft.

Dann *ab:* die blanke Haube eines Helden,
Mittschiffs aufgebahrt über schießendem Wasser.

Ab, als Variante: Ein Spielzeug aus Licht,
Durch ihn stromauf gespult, in nichts verfangen.

In Memoriam: Robert Fitzgerald

The socket of each axehead like the squared
Doorway to a megalithic tomb
With its slabbed passage that keeps opening forward
To face another corbelled stone-faced door
That opens on a third. There is no last door,
Just threshold stone, stone jambs, stone crossbeam
Repeating *enter, enter, enter, enter.*
Lintel and upright fly past in the dark.

After the bowstring sang a swallow's note,
The arrow whose migration is its mark
Leaves a whispered breath in every socket.
The great test over, while the gut's still humming,
This time it travels out of all knowing
Perfectly aimed towards the vacant centre.

In memoriam Robert Fitzgerald

Das Öhr von jeder Axt wie das Quadrat
Des Eingangstors zu einem Hünengrab,
Plattenbelegt, sich ständig vorwärts öffnend
Auf ein weiteres gekragtes Steingesicht von Tor,
Das auf ein drittes geht. Es gibt kein letztes Tor,
Nur Schwellenstein, Stein-Pfosten, Stein-Querbalken,
Ein wiederholtes *komm, tritt ein, tritt ein.*
Leibung und Sturz schießen vorbei im Dunkel.

Die Sehne hat ein Schwalbenlied gesungen.
Der Pfeil, für den die Wanderung das Ziel ist,
Läßt einen Flüsterhauch in jedem Öhr zurück.
Vorbei die Prüfung. Noch versummt die Saite,
Und diesmal fliegt er jenseits allen Wissens,
Vollkommen ausgerichtet nach dem leeren Zentrum.

The Old Team

Dusk. Scope of air. A railed pavilion
Formal and blurring in the sepia
Of (always) summery Edwardian
Ulster. Which could be India
Or England. Or any old parade ground
Where a moustachioed tenantry togged out
To pose with folded arms, all musclebound
And staunch and forever up against it.

Moyola Park FC! Sons of Castledawson!
Stokers and scutchers! Grandfather McCann!
Team spirit, walled parkland, the linen mill
Have, in your absence, grown historical
As those lightly clapped, dull-thumping games of football.
The steady coffins sail past at eye-level.

Die alte Mannschaft

Abendlicht. Raume Luft. Ein Pavillon beinah,
Förmlich und unbestimmt im sepiabraunen,
(grundsätzlich) sommerlichen »guten alten«
Ulster. Es könnte auch Indien sein, ja
England. Oder sonstein beliebiger Exerzier-
platz, wo schnauzbärtige Pächter aufmarschierten,
Im Sonntagsstaat, Arme verschränkt, mit Muskelkater
Und zuverlässig und ständig vor der Pleite.

Moyola Park FC! Söhne von Castledawson!
Heizer und Schwinger! Großvater McCann!
Teamgeist, ummauerte Parks, Flachs-Spinnerei
Sind, seit ihr fort seid, obsolet geworden
Wie jene dünn beklatschten, dumpfen Bolzereien.
Die endlosen Särge ziehen in Augenhöhe vorbei.

Clearances

in memoriam M. K. H., 1911-1984

She taught me what her uncle once taught her:
How easily the biggest coal block split
If you got the grain and hammer angled right.

The sound of that relaxed alluring blow,
Its co-opted and obliterated echo,
Taught me to hit, taught me to loosen,

Taught me between the hammer and the block
To face the music. Teach me now to listen,
To strike it rich behind the linear black.

Lichtungen

in memoriam M. K. H., 1911-1984

Sie lehrte mich, was ihr Onkel sie einst lehrte:
Wie leicht der größte Kohleblock zerbrach,
Wenn nur das Korn richtig zum Hammer lag.

Dieser entspannte zauberische Knall,
Sein kooptierter und verdeckter Nachhall
Lehrten mich zu schlagen, loszulassen,

Lehrten mich, zwischen dem Hammer und dem Block, mich
Der Musik zu stellen. Lehren mich jetzt zu lauschen,
Den Kern zu treffen hinter schwarzem Strich.

I

A cobble thrown a hundred years ago
Keeps coming at me, the first stone
Aimed at a great-grandmother's turncoat brow.
The pony jerks and the riot's on.
She's crouched low in the trap
Running the gauntlet that first Sunday
Down the brae to Mass at a panicked gallop.
He whips on through the town to cries of ›Lundy!‹

Call her ›The Convert‹. ›The Exogamous Bride‹.
Anyhow, it is a genre piece
Inherited on my mother's side
And mine to dispose with now she's gone.
Instead of silver and Victorian lace,
The exonerating, exonerated stone.

I

Ein Stein, den man vor hundert Jahren warf,
Kommt auf mich zu: der erste Pflasterstein,
Der einer Urgroßmutter Überläuferstirn galt.
Das Pferd geht durch, das Chaos wird allgemein.
Sie macht sich klein am Boden des Gefährts,
Spießrutenlauf an jenem ersten Sonntag,
In wilder Jagd zur Messe, hügelabwärts.
Er peitscht sich durch die wild gewordene Stadt.

Nennt sie »Die Exogame Braut«. »Die Konvertitin«.
Jedenfalls ist es ein Genre-Stück,
Erbteil von meiner Mutter Seite
Und, da sie tot ist, nun in meinen Händen.
Statt viktorianischer Spitzen oder Schmuck:
Der Stein, entbindend und entbunden.

2

Polished linoleum shone there. Brass taps shone.
The china cups were very white and big –
An unchipped set with sugar bowl and jug.
The kettle whistled. Sandwich and teascone
Were present and correct. In case it run,
The butter must be kept out of the sun.
And don't be dropping crumbs. Don't tilt your chair.
Don't reach. Don't point. Don't make noise when you stir.

It is Number 5, New Row, Land of the Dead,
Where grandfather is rising from his place
With spectacles pushed back on a clean bald head
To welcome a bewildered homing daughter
Before she even knocks. ›What's this? What's this?‹
And they sit down in the shining room together.

2

Linoleum glänzte dort. Messinge Hähne glänzten.
Die porzellanenen Tassen waren sehr weiß und groß –
Ein unversehrtes, vollständiges Service.
Der Kessel pfiff. Rosinenbrot und Schnitten
Waren da und wie sich's gehört. Jedes Kind begreift,
Daß Butter in der Sonne leicht zerläuft.
Und krümel nicht. Halt deine Beine still.
Rühr leise um. Man fragt, wenn man was will.

Es ist New Row Nummer 5, im Land der Toten –
Großvater erhebt sich grad von seinem Platz,
Die Brille auf die Glatze hochgeschoben,
Um eine heimgekehrte Tochter zu empfangen,
Noch ehe sie, staunend, anklopft: »Was ist das?«
Und sitzen dann im hellen Raum beisammen.

3

When all the others were away at Mass
I was all hers as we peeled potatoes.
They broke the silence, let fall one by one
Like solder weeping off the soldering iron:
Cold comforts set between us, things to share
Gleaming in a bucket of clean water.
And again let fall. Little pleasant splashes
From each other's work would bring us to our senses.

So while the parish priest at her bedside
Went hammer and tongs at the prayers for the dying
And some were responding and some crying
I remembered her head bent towards my head,
Her breath in mine, our fluent dipping knives –
Never closer the whole rest of our lives.

3

Wenn alle anderen fort zur Messe waren,
Gehörte ich ganz ihr beim Kartoffelschälen.
Sie brachen das Schweigen, einzeln fallengelassen
Wie Lötzinn-Tropfen, die vom Kolben tränen:
Magerer Trost, der zwischen uns stand, Gemeinsamkeiten,
Schimmernd in einem Eimer klaren Wassers.
Und wieder fallengelassen. Frische kleine
Gluckslaute, die uns zur Besinnung brachten.

So sah ich, als der Pfarrer an ihrer Seite
Sterbegebete wie ein Wilder rezitierte,
Und manche weinten, manche respondierten,
Wieder ihren Kopf, der sich zu meinem neigte,
Ihren Hauch in meinem, die flinken nassen Klingen –
Nichts konnte uns je einander näher bringen.

4

Fear of affectation made her affect
Inadequacy whenever it came to
Pronouncing words ›beyond her‹. *Bertold Brek*.
She'd manage something hampered and askew
Every time, as if she might betray
The hampered and inadequate by too
Well-adjusted a vocabulary.
With more challenge than pride, she'd tell me, ›You
Know all them things.‹ So I governed my tongue
In front of her, a genuinely well-
adjusted adequate betrayal
Of what I knew better. I'd *naw* and *aye*
And decently relapse into the wrong
Grammar which kept us allied and at bay.

4

Aus Angst vor Affektiertheit affektierte
Sie Unzulänglichkeit, wenn sie sich gedrängt
Fühlte, »Gelehrtes« auszusprechen. *Schammpol Sarter.*
Sie brachte es immer schief und irgendwie beschränkt
Zustande, als ob sie sonst, durch einen zu
Passenden Wortschatz, die Beschränkte
Und Unzulängliche verraten hätte.
Eher vorwurfsvoll als stolz hieß es dann: »Du
Weißt ja sowas.« So brauchte ich Sprachgefühl,
Im Umgang mit ihr – einen in der Tat
Zulänglich passenden Verrat
An meinem besseren Wissen. Und ich verfiel
Rücksichtsvoll wieder in das Platt,
Das uns auf gleicher Stufe und in Schach hielt.

5

The cool that came off sheets just off the line
Made me think the damp must still be in them
But when I took my corners of the linen
And pulled against her, first straight down the hem
And then diagonally, then flapped and shook
The fabric like a sail in a cross-wind,
They made a dried-out undulating thwack.
So we'd stretch and fold and end up hand to hand
For a split second as if nothing had happened
For nothing had that had not always happened
Beforehand, day by day, just touch and go,
Coming close again by holding back
In moves where I was x and she was o
Inscribed in sheets she'd sewn from ripped-out flour sacks.

5

Die Frische von frisch abgenommenen Laken
Ließ mich erst glauben, sie seien noch etwas klamm,
Doch faßte ich dann das Stück an meinen Ecken,
Und zog von ihr weg, erst der Länge nach,
Dann diagonal, und schüttelte die Leinwand
Wie ein Segel, wenn der Wind sich plötzlich dreht,
Knallten sie flatternd, durch und durch getrocknet.
So spannten, falteten wir – Hand an Hand
Für einen Augenblick, als sei gar nichts geschehen,
Denn es war nur Alltägliches geschehen,
Schon längst Gehabtes: angerührt wegschrecken
Und, an sich haltend, dann auch wieder nah,
So, Zug um Zug, wo ich das X und sie das O war,
Gedruckt auf Laken aus aufgetrennten Mehlsäcken.

6

In the first flush of the Easter holidays
The ceremonies during Holy Week
Were highpoints of our *Sons and Lovers* phase.
The midnight fire. The paschal candlestick.
Elbow to elbow, glad to be kneeling next
To each other up there near the front
Of the packed church, we would follow the text
And rubrics for the blessing of the font.
As the hind longs for the streams, so my soul . . .
Dippings. Towellings. The water breathed on.
The water mixed with chrism and with oil.
Cruet tinkle. Formal incensation
And the psalmist's outcry taken up with pride:
Day and night my tears have been my bread.

6

Im allerersten Glanz der Osterferien
Waren die Zeremonien der Heiligen Woche
Höhepunkte unserer *Söhne und Liebhaber*-Epoche.
Das Mitternachtsfeuer. Der Osterkerzenständer.
Ellbogennah, glücklich, zu knien nächst
Dem anderen, ganz vorn, fast in der ersten Reihe
Der überfüllten Kirche, folgten wir dem Text
Und den Rubriken für die Taufsteinweihe.
Wie der Hirsch lechzt nach frischem Naß . . .
Eintauchen. Trockenreiben. Das Wasser und der Hauch.
Mit Chrisam und mit Öl vermischtes Wasser.
Meßgeschirrklirren. Feierlicher Weihrauch
Und der Psalm-Aufschrei, der unseren Stolz entfacht:
Tränen waren mein Brot bei Tag und Nacht.

7

In the last minutes he said more to her
Almost than in all their life together.
›You'll be in New Row on Monday night
And I'll come up for you and you'll be glad
When I walk in the door . . . Isn't that right?‹
His head was bent down to her propped-up head.
She could not hear but we were overjoyed.
He called her good and girl. Then she was dead,
The searching for a pulsebeat was abandoned
And we all knew one thing by being there.
The space we stood around had been emptied
Into us to keep, it penetrated
Clearances that suddenly stood open.
High cries were felled and a pure change happened.

7

In den letzten Minuten sagte er ihr mehr,
Beinah, als in ihrem ganzen Leben vorher.
»Am Montag abend bist du in New Row,
Und dann ich hol dich ab, und du bist froh,
Wenn ich zu dir hereinkomm . . . Oder nicht?«
Sein Kopf geneigt zu ihrem aufgestützten Kopf.
Sie hörte nichts mehr, doch wir waren selig.
Er nannte sie gut und Kind. Dann war sie tot,
Die Suche nach dem Puls wurde aufgegeben,
Und alle, wie wir da waren, wußten eines.
Der Raum, um den wir standen, war geleert
Und in uns aufgehoben, er erfüllte
Lichtungen, die plötzlich offenstanden.
Schreie zerbarsten, und es geschah ein reiner Wandel.

8

I thought of walking round and round a space
Utterly empty, utterly a source
Where the decked chestnut tree had lost its place
In our front hedge above the wallflowers.
The white chips jumped and jumped and skited high.
I heard the hatchet's differentiated
Accurate cut, the crack, the sigh
And collapse of what luxuriated
Through the shocked tips and wreckage of it all.
Deep planted and long gone, my coeval
Chestnut from a jam jar in a hole,
Its heft and hush become a bright nowhere,
A soul ramifying and forever
Silent, beyond silence listened for.

8

Ich wollte Kreis um Kreis ziehen rund um einen Raum,
Vollkommen leer, vollkommen eine Quelle,
Wo früher der leuchtende Kastanienbaum
In unserer Hecke, bei dem Goldlack seine Stelle
Gehabt hatte. Die weißen Späne hüpften, spritzten quer.
Ich hörte den differenzierten, sehr exakten
Einschlag des Beils, den Knall, den Seufzer
Und Sturz des Wüchsigen durch die geschockten
Spitzen und den völligen Ruin.
Tief gepflanzt und längst fort, mit mir gediehen,
Mein Baum aus einem Weckglas in ein Loch,
Seine Wucht und Stille werden ein helles Nirgends,
Eine Seele, sich verästelnd und für immer
Schweigend, jenseits des Schweigens, das man sucht.

The Milk Factory

Scuts of froth swirled from the discharge pipe.
We halted on the other bank and watched
A milky water run from the pierced side
Of milk itself, the crock of its substance spilt
Across white limbo floors where shift-workers
Waded round the clock, and the factory
Kept its distance like a bright-decked star-ship.

There we go, soft-eyed calves of the dew,
Astonished and assumed into fluorescence.

Die Milchfabrik

Schaumbüschel schwirrten aus dem Abflußrohr.
Wir hielten am anderen Ufer an und sahen
Milchiges Wasser aus der durchbohrten Seite
Der Milch selbst laufen, der Schorf ihrer Substanz
Spritzte über weiße Limbus-Böden, wo Schichtarbeiter
Rund um die Uhr wateten, und die Fabrik
Hielt Abstand wie ein hellgedecktes Sternschiff.

Und weg sind wir, sanftäugige Kälber des Taus,
Erstaunt und in den Fluorglanz aufgenommen.

The Summer of Lost Rachel

Potato crops are flowering,
    Hard green plums appear
On damson trees at your back door
    And every berried briar

Is glittering and dripping
    Whenever showers plout down
On flooded hay and flooding drills.
    There's a ring around the moon.

The whole summer was waterlogged
    Yet everyone is loath
To trust the rain's soft-soaping ways
    And sentiments of growth

Because all confidence in summer's
    Unstinting largesse
Broke down last May when we laid you out
    In white, your whited face

Gashed from the accident, but still,
    So absolutely still,
And the setting sun set merciless
    And every merciful

Register inside us yearned
    To run the film back,
For you to step into the road
    Wheeling your bright-rimmed bike,

Safe and sound as usual,
    Across, then down the lane,
The twisted spokes all straightened out,
    The awful skid-marks gone.

Der Sommer der verlorenen Rahel

Kartoffelpflanzen stehen in Blüte,
    Hart-grün blinken Zwetschgen
An Bäumen hinter deinem Haus,
    Und jede Rosenhecke

In Frucht funkelt und trieft,
    Sooft ein Schauer strömt
Und Heu und Furchen überschwemmt.
    Ein Hof ist um den Mond.

Der ganze Sommer war durchweicht,
    Doch niemand hat noch Lust,
Den Regen-Schmeicheleien zu trauen,
    Der froh geschwellten Brust,

Weil jeder Glaube an des Sommers
    Gabenreiche Pracht
Letzten Mai schwand, als wir dich in Weiß
    Aufbahrten, dein Gesicht

Vom Unfall aufgeschlitzt, doch still,
    So ganz vollkommen stille,
Und mitleidlos die Sonne sank,
    Und jedes mitleidvolle

Register in uns verlangte
    Nach einem neuen Start,
Daß du dann auf die Straße trittst
    Mit deinem blanken Rad,

Heil und gesund wie eh und je,
    Hinüber, dann ums Eck,
Die krummen Speichen wieder grad,
    Die schlimme Schleifspur weg.

But no. So let the downpours flood
    Our memory's riverbed
Until, in thick-webbed currents,
    The life you might have led

Wavers and tugs dreamily
    As soft-plumed waterweed
Which tempts our gaze and quietens it
    And recollects our need.

Doch nein. So mag der Regen unser
    Gedächtnis überfluten,
Bis in verwobnen Strömungen
    Dein ungelebtes Leben

Träumerisch zerrt und flattert
    Wie weiche Wassermyrthe,
Die unseren Blick versucht und stillt
    Und unsere Not erinnert.

The Wishing Tree

I thought of her as the wishing tree that died
And saw it lifted, root and branch, to heaven,
Trailing a shower of all that had been driven

Need by need by need into its hale
Sap-wood and bark: coin and pin and nail
Came streaming from it like a comet-tail

New-minted and dissolved. I had a vision
Of an airy branch-head rising through damp cloud,
Of turned-up faces where the tree had stood.

Der Wunschbaum

Ich sah in ihr den Baum der Wünsche – tot
Und in den Himmel, Stumpf und Stiel, gehoben,
Behängt mit einem Schwall von allem, was bis eben

Not um Not um Not in seine Kraft,
Splintholz und Borke trieb: Geldstück, Nadel, Stift
Entströmten ihm wie ein Kometenschaft,

Neugemünzt und zergangen. Ich hatte eine Vision –
Ein hohes Zweig-Haupt steigt durch feuchte Wolkenwand
Aufschauender Gesichter, wo der Baum sonst stand.

A Postcard from Iceland

As I dipped to test the stream some yards away
From a hot spring, I could hear nothing
But the whole mud-slick muttering and boiling.

And then my guide behind me saying,
›Lukewarm. And I think you'd want to know
That *luk* was an old Icelandic word for hand.‹

And you would want to know (but you know already)
How usual that waft and pressure felt
When the inner palm of water found my palm.

Eine Postkarte aus Island

Als ich kurz ins Wasser griff, nur ein paar Meter
Von einer heißen Quelle, konnte ich gar nichts hören
Außer dem ganzen schlammigen Geblubber.

Und dann den Führer hinter mir, der sagte:
»Lauwarm. Und es wird Sie interessieren,
Daß *lau* auf altisländisch ›Hand‹ bedeutete.«

Und dich wird interessieren (doch du weißt es schon),
Wie alltäglich dieser gehauchte Druck sich anfühlte,
Als die innere Hand des Wassers meine fand.

A Peacock's Feather

for Daisy Garnett

Six days ago the water fell
To christen you, to work its spell
And wipe your slate, we hope, for good.
But now your life is sleep and food
Which, with the touch of love, suffice
You, Daisy, Daisy, English niece.

Gloucestershire: its prospects lie
Wooded and misty to my eye
Whose landscape, as your mother's was,
Is other than this mellowness
Of topiary, lawn and brick,
Possessed, untrespassed, walled, nostalgic.

I come from scraggy farm and moss,
Old patchworks that the pitch and toss
Of history have left dishevelled.
But here, for your sake, I have levelled
My cart-track voice to garden tones,
Cobbled the bog with Cotswold stones.

Ravelling strands of families mesh
In love-knots of two minds, one flesh.
The future's not our own. We'll weave
An in-law maze, we'll nod and wave
With trust but little intimacy –
So this is a billet-doux to say

That in a warm July you lay
Christened and smiling in Bradley
While I, a guest in your green court,
At a west window sat and wrote

Eine Pfauenfeder

für Daisy Garnett

Sechs Tage, seit das Wasser rann,
Dich taufte und seinen Zauberbann
Wirkte, um die Erbschuld ganz zu streichen.
(Wir hoffen's.) Doch einstweilen reichen
Dir Liebe, Schlaf und Milchgerichte,
Englische Daisy, kleine Nichte.

Die Aussichten von Gloucestershire,
Waldig, verschleiert, liegen mir
Vor Augen, dessen Landschaft (auch
Die deiner Mutter) nicht Zierstrauch,
Gepflegter Rasen, Backstein war –
Besessen, ungestört und unverlierbar.

Ich komme aus kargem Land, bemoost,
Gestoppelt, vom Herumgeschiebe
Unsrer Geschichte arg verwahrlost.
Aber hier hab ich, dir zuliebe,
Meine Ackerstimme sanft gemacht,
Das Moor mit Rosen überdacht.

Lose Familien-Enden binden
Knoten der Liebe: ein Fleisch, zwei Seelen.
Die Zukunft ist uns fremd. Wir finden
Uns verwandt, können aufeinander zählen,
Vertrauensvoll doch nicht sehr nah.
Deshalb dies Briefchen – es sagt: Da

Lagst du in der Wärme des Julei,
Getauft und lächelnd in Bradley,
Dieweil ich, Gast in deinem Haus,
Am Fenster saß (nach Westen raus)

Self-consciously in gathering dark.
I might as well be in Coole Park.

So before I leave your ordered home,
Let us pray. May tilth and loam,
Darkened with Celts' and Saxons' blood,
Breastfeed your love of house and wood –
Where I drop this for you, as I pass,
Like the peacock's feather on the grass.

1972

Und schrieb, befangen. Dunkel stellt sich ein.
Ich könnt genausogut in Coole Park sein.

Ehe ich nun also Abschied nehm',
Wollen wir beten. Möge durch Land und Lehm,
Dunkel vom Blut von Kelten und von Sachsen,
Deine Liebe zu Haus und Wäldern wachsen –
Wo ich dies hier im Vorbeigehn fallen laß
Wie die Pfauenfeder auf das Gras.

1972

Grotus and Coventina

Far from home Grotus dedicated an altar to Coventina
Who holds in her right hand a waterweed
And in her left a pitcher spilling out a river.
Anywhere Grotus looked at running water he felt at home
And when he remembered the stone where he cut his name
Some dried-up course beneath his breastbone started
Pouring and darkening – more or less the way
The thought of his stunted altar works on me.

Remember when our electric pump gave out,
Priming it with bucketfuls, our idiotic rage
And hangdog phone-calls to the farm next door
For somebody please to come and fix it?
And when it began to hammer on again,
Jubilation at the tap's full force, the sheer
Given fact of water, how you felt you'd never
Waste one drop but know its worth better always.
Do you think we could run through all that one more time?
I'll be Grotus, you be Coventina.

Grotus und Coventina

Fern von daheim weihte Grotus einen Altar der Coventina,
Die in der Rechten eine Wassermyrthe hält
Und links ein Krüglein, einen Fluß vergießend.
Wo immer Grotus Wasser rinnen sah, fühlte er sich heimisch,
Und wenn er des Steines gedachte, der seinen Namen trug,
Begann etwas Versiegtes unter seinem Brustbein
Dunkelnd zu strömen – fast wie der Gedanke
An seinen dürftigen Altar jetzt auf mich wirkt.

Weißt du noch, als unsere Elektropumpe stehenblieb,
Die Eimer, die wir schleppten, unsere blöde Wut
Und die zerknirschten Anrufe nach dem Nachbarhof,
Daß bitte jemand käm, um sie zu richten?
Und als das Stampfen endlich wieder losging,
Den Jubel ob des vollen Drucks vom Rohr, der bloßen
Gegebenheit des Wassers, die Gewißheit, daß man's nie mehr
Vergeuden, es fürderhin zu schätzen wissen würde.
Meinst du, wir könnten das Ganze noch einmal durchspielen?
Ich bin dann Grotus, sei du Coventina.

Coventina ist im zweiten Jahrhundert n. Chr. als Göttin einer Heilquelle
bezeugt. Aurelius Crotus Germanus, den Heaney Grotus nennt, hat für ihr
Standbild einen Sockel gestiftet.

Holding Course

Propellers underwater, cabins drumming, lights –
Unthought-of but constant out there every night,
The big ferries pondered on their courses.
I envy you your sight of them this morning,
Docked and massive with their sloped-back funnels.

The outlook is high and airy where you stand
By our attic window. Far Toledo blues.
And from a shelf behind you
The alpine thistle we brought from Covadonga
Inclines its jaggy crest.

Last autumn we were smouldering and parched
As those spikes that keep vigil overhead
Like Grendel's steely talon nailed
To the mead-hall roof. And then we broke through
Or we came through. It was its own reward.

We are voluptuaries of the morning after.
As gulls cry out above the deep channels
And you stand on and on, twiddling your hair,
Think of me as your MacWhirr of the boudoir,
Head on, one track, ignorant of manœuvre.

Auf Kurs bleiben

Propeller unter Wasser, Dröhn-Kabinen, Lichter –
Unbeachtet doch beständig jede Nacht da draußen,
Wägten die großen Fähren ihren Kurs ab.
Ich neid dir ihren Anblick heute morgen,
Vertäut und wuchtig, schräggeneigten Schornsteins.

Hohe, ungetrübte Aussicht hast du da,
Aus unserer Mansarde. Fernes Toledoblau.
Und hinter dir, vom Bord, neigt
Die Silberdistel, die wir in Covadonga pflückten,
Ihren gezackten Helm.

Wir schwelten letzten Herbst, waren ausgedörrt
Wie diese Stacheln, wachend über uns
Gleich Grendels eherner Klaue, festgenagelt
Ans Dach der Met-Halle. Und dann brachen wir durch,
Oder kamen durch. Es trug in sich den Lohn.

Wir sind Wollüstlinge des Morgens nach der Nacht.
Während Möwen über den Fahrrinnen schreien,
Und du so stehst und stehst, an Strähnen zwirbelnd –
Denk an mich als deinen MacWhirr des Boudoirs,
Stur, gradheraus, keines Manövers fähig.

The Song of the Bullets

I watched a long time in the yard
    The usual stars, the still
And seemly planets, lantern-bright
    Above our darkened hill.

And then a star that moved, I thought,
    For something moved indeed
Up from behind the massed skyline
    At ardent silent speed

And when it reached the zenith, cut
    Across the curving path
Of a second light that swung up like
    A scythe-point through its swathe.

›The sky at night is full of us‹,
    Now one began to sing,
›Our slugs of lead lie cold and dead,
    Our trace is on the wing.

Our casings and our blunted parts
    Are gathered up below
As justice stands aghast and stares
    Like the sun on arctic snow.

Our guilt was accidental. Blame,
    Blame because you must.
Then blame young men for semen or
    Blame the moon for moondust.‹

As ricochets that warble close,
    Then die away on wind,
That hard contralto sailed across
    And stellar quiet reigned

Das Lied der Geschosse

Ich stand lang, und ich sah, im Hof,
    Gewohnte Sterne funkeln,
Still-schöne Welten, lampenhell,
    Und unseren Hügel dunkeln.

Dann einen Stern, dacht ich, der flog,
    Denn etwas flog nun doch,
Jenseits des schwarzen Horizonts,
    Glühend und lautlos hoch,

Und wie es den Zenit erreichte,
    Schnitt es die Kurvenbahn
Eines zweiten Lichts, das aufwärts wie
    Eine Sensenspitze kam.

»Nachts ist der Himmel voll von uns«,
    Fing eines an zu singen,
»Unsere Bleigestalt liegt tot und kalt,
    Wenn wir uns höherschwingen.

Unsere Hülsen, unsere stumpfen Teile
    Sammelt man auf mit Fleiß,
Während Justitia entgeistert starrt
    Wie die Sonne auf ewiges Eis.

Unsere Schuld war Zufall. Wirf
    Sie uns, da du mußt, nur vor.
Wirf Burschen dann ihr Sperma, wirf
    Dem Mond den Mondstaub vor.«

Wie ein Prellschuß erst ganz nahe zwitschert
    Und dann im Wind versumnt,
Flog dieser harte Alt vorüber.
    Dann schwieg das Sternenrund,

Until the other fireball spoke:
    We are the iron will.
We hoop and cooper worlds beyond
    The killer and the kill.

Mont Olivet's beatitudes,
    The soul's cadenced desires
Cannot prevail against us who
    Dwell in the marbled fires

Of every steady eye that ever
    Narrowed, sighted, paused:
We fire and glaze the shape of things
    Until the shape's imposed.‹

Now wind was blowing through the yard.
    Clouds blanked the stars. The still
And seemly planets disappeared
    Above our darkened hill.

Bis die andere Feuerkugel sprach:
»Wir sind der eherne Wille.
Wir umfassen ganze Welten, nicht
Nur den Töter und sein Wild.

Die Seligpreisungen des Ölbergs,
　　Der Seele rhythmisch Sehnen
Vermögen gar nichts gegen uns,
　　Die im kalten Feuer wohnen

Jedes ruhigen Auges, das sich je
　　verengte, zielte – und steht:
Wir glühen, glasieren jede Form,
　　Bis Form zum Zwang gerät.«

Jetzt war es windig auf dem Hof.
　　Umwölkt das Sterngefunkel.
Die schönen Welten schwanden still
　　Über dem Hügeldunkel.

Wolfe Tone

Light as a skiff, manoeuvrable
yet outmanoeuvred,

I affected epaulettes and a cockade,
wrote a style well-bred and impervious

to the solidarity I angled for,
and played the ancient Roman with a razor.

I was the shouldered oar that ended up
far from the brine and whiff of venture,

like a scratching-post or a crossroads flagpole,
out of my element among small farmers –

I who once wakened to the shouts of men
rising from the bottom of the sea,

men in their shirts mounting through deep water
when the Atlantic stove our cabin's dead lights in

and the big fleet split and Ireland dwindled
as we ran before the gale under bare poles.

Wolfe Tone

Leicht wie ein Skiff, manövrierfähig
doch ausmanövriert,

schmückte ich mich mit Epauletts, einer Kokarde,
schrieb mit gutem Stil und ohne Sinn

für die Fraternité, auf die ich aus war,
und spielte alter Römer mit dem Messer.

Ich war das Ruder, das, geschultert, fern
von See und Hauch von Abenteuer endet,

wie ein Scheuerpfosten oder Pfahl am Kreuzweg,
Fisch auf dem Trockenen unter kleinen Bauern –

ich, der ich einst von Männerschreien erwachte,
Männer schrien herauf vom Meeresgrund,

Männer im Hemd, im tiefen Wasser steigend,
als der Atlantik unsere Kajüte sprengte

und die Flotte zerfiel und Irland hinschwand –
segelnd vor Topp und Takel vor dem Sturm.

A Shooting Script

They are riding away from whatever might have been
Towards what will never be, in a held shot:
Teachers on bicycles, saluting native speakers,
Treading the nineteen-twenties like the future.

Still pedalling out at the end of the lens,
Not getting anywhere and not getting away.
Mix to fuchsia that ›follows the language‹.
A long soundless sequence. Pan and fade.

Then voices over, in different Irishes,
Discussing translation jobs and rates per line;
Like nineteenth-century milestones in grass verges,
Occurrence of names like R. M. Ballantyne.

A close-up on the cat's eye of a button
Pulling back wide to the cape of a soutane,
Biretta, Roman collar, Adam's apple.
Freeze his blank face. Let the credits run

And just when it looks as if it is all over –
Tracking shots of a long wave up a strand
That breaks towards the point of a stick writing and writing
Words in the old script in the running sand.

Ein Exposé

Sie fahren weg, von was immer hätte sein können,
Auf etwas zu, das nie sein wird, in der Totalen:
Lehrer auf Fahrrädern, die Muttersprachler grüßen,
Stramm durch die Zwanziger, als ob's die Zukunft wäre.

Sie radeln noch, schon am Rand des Suchers,
Und kommen nirgendhin und nicht vom Fleck.
Bildmischung auf Fuchsie, »analog zur Sprache«.
Lange stumme Sequenz. Dann Schwenk und ab.

Dann Stimmen off, die unterschiedlich irisch
Übersetzungsjobs erörtern, Honorare;
Wie viktorianische Meilensteine auf Grasstreifen
Sind Namen wie R. M. Ballantyne eingestreut.

Großaufnahme: das Katzenauge eines Knopfes,
Zurückziehen auf halbnah: das Cape einer Soutane,
Birett, römischer Kragen, Adamsapfel.
Die leere Miene einfrieren. Abspann laufen lassen,

Und grade, wenn man meint, das sei das Ende –
Fahrtaufnahmen einer langen Welle, einen Strand
Hinauf, bis hin zu einem Stock, der schreibt und schreibt,
Worte in der alten Schrift in den fliehenden Sand.

From the Canton of Expectation

I

We lived deep in a land of optative moods,
under high, banked clouds of resignation.
A rustle of loss in the phrase *Not in our lifetime*,
the broken nerve when we prayed *Vouchsafe* or *Deign*,
were creditable, sufficient to the day.

Once a year we gathered in a field
of dance platforms and tents where children sang
songs they had learned by rote in the old language.
An auctioneer who had fought in the brotherhood
enumerated the humiliations
we always took for granted, but not even he
considered this, I think, a call to action.
Iron-mouthed loudspeakers shook the air
yet nobody felt blamed. He had confirmed us.
When our rebel anthem played the meeting shut
we turned for home and the usual harassment
by militiamen on overtime at roadblocks.

II

And next thing, suddenly, this change of mood.
Books open in the newly-wired kitchens.
Young heads that might have dozed a life away
against the flanks of milking cows were busy
paving and pencilling their first causeways
across the prescribed texts. The paving stones
of quadrangles came next and a grammar
of imperatives, the new age of demands.
They would banish the conditional for ever,
this generation born impervious to

Aus dem Kanton der Erwartung

I

Wir lebten tief in einem Land der Wunschform,
unter hohen Wolkenbänken der Ergebung.
Ein Rascheln von Verlust in *Nicht in unserm Leben*,
die Zagheit unseres *HErr, gewähre* und *Neige*
waren lobenswert, hatten soweit gereicht.

Einmal im Jahr vereinte uns ein Feld
von Tanzböden und Zelten, sangen Kinder
auswendig Lieder in der alten Sprache.
Ein Auktionator, ehemals Freiheitskämpfer,
zählte uns die Entwürdigungen auf,
die wir nie hinterfragten; doch nicht einmal er
schien dies als Ruf zum Handeln aufzufassen.
Lautsprecherstahl erschütterte die Luft,
doch niemand schämte sich. Er hatte uns bestätigt.
War die Versammlung kämpferisch verklungen,
begannen Heimfahrt und übliche Schikanen
an Straßensperren mit eifrigen Milizen.

II

Und dann, ganz plötzlich, dieser Stimmungswechsel.
Offne Bücher in den Küchen, jetzt mit Strom.
Junge Köpfe, die ein Leben an den Flanken
von Milchkühen hätten verschlafen können,
pflasterten strichelnd Ihre ersten Bahnen
durch vorgeschriebenen Text. Die Pflastersteine
der Kästchen folgten und eine Grammatik
der Imperative: Die neue Zeit *verlangte*.
Sie wollte auf ewig den Konditional verbannen,
diese Generation, geboren ohne Sinn

the triumph in our cries of *de profundis*.
Our faith in winning by enduring most
they made anathema, intelligences
brightened and unmannerly as crowbars.

III

What looks the strongest has outlived its term.
The future lies with what's affirmed from under.
These things that corroborated us when we dwelt
under the aegis of our stealthy patron,
the guardian angel of passivity,
now sink a fang of menace in my shoulder.
I repeat the word ›stricken‹ to myself
and stand bareheaded under the banked clouds
edged more and more with brassy thunderlight.
I yearn for hammerblows on clinkered planks,
the uncompromised report of driven thole-pins,
to know there is one among us who never swerved
from all his instincts told him was right action,
who stood his ground in the indicative,
whose boat will lift when the cloudburst happens.

für den Triumph in unsren Rufen *de profundis*.
Unseren Glauben an den Sieg des Dulders
nannten sie Ketzerei – Geister, geschärft
und rücksichtslos wie Äxte.

III

Was scheinbar herrscht, hat sich schon überlebt.
Zukunft empfängt von unten die Bestimmung.
All das, was uns bestärkte, als wir unter
der Obhut unseres verstohlenen Schutzherrn
lebten, des Engels der Passivität,
bohrt mir nun drohende Fänge in die Schulter.
Ich wiederhol das Wort »geschlagen« vor mich hin
und stehe barhäuptig unter Wolkenbänken,
zunehmend verbrämt mit grellem Wetterstrahl.
Ich lechz nach Hammerschlag auf Klinkerplanken,
dem unbeugsamen Laut getriebener Dollen,
danach, zu wissen, unter uns gibt's einen,
der nie von all dem abließ, was sein Fühlen
als rechtes Handeln wies, der kompromißlos
im Indikativ blieb, dessen Boot steigen
wird, wenn die Wolken bersten.

The Mud Vision

Statues with exposed hearts and barbed-wire crowns
Still stood in alcoves, hares flitted beneath
The dozing bellies of jets, our menu-writers
And punks with aerosol sprays held their own
With the best of them. Satellite link-ups
Wafted over us the blessings of popes, heliports
Maintained a charmed circle for idols on tour
And casualties on their stretchers. We sleepwalked
The line between panic and formulae, screentested
Our first native models and the last of the mummers,
Watching ourselves at a distance, advantaged
And airy as a man on a springboard
Who keeps limbering up because the man cannot dive.

And then in the foggy midlands it appeared,
Our mud vision, as if a rose window of mud
Had invented itself out of the glittery damp,
A gossamer wheel, concentric with its own hub
Of nebulous dirt, sullied yet lucent.
We had heard of the sun standing still and the sun
That changed colour, but we were vouchsafed
Original clay, transfigured and spinning.
And then the sunsets ran murky, the wiper
Could never entirely clean off the windscreen,
Reservoirs tasted of silt, a light fuzz
Accrued in the hair and the eyebrows, and some
Took to wearing a smudge on their foreheads
To be prepared for whatever. Vigils
Began to be kept around puddled gaps,
On altars bulrushes ousted the lilies
And a rota of invalids came and went
On beds they could lease placed in range of the shower.

Die Schlammvision

Statuen mit offenem Herzen und Stacheldrahtkronen
Besetzten noch Nischen, Hasen huschten unter
Dösenden Bäuchen von Jets, unsre Menüdichter
Und Spraydosen-Punks behaupteten sich
Mit allem was drin war. Satellitenverbindungen
Wehten die Segen von Päpsten herab, Heliports
Hielten einen Bannkreis aufrecht für Idole auf Tour
Und Opfer auf ihren Bahren. Wir schlafwandelten
Auf dem Grat zwischen Panik und Phrasen, machten
Probeaufnahmen unserer ersten einheimischen Models
Und des allerletzten Mimen, schauten uns dabei selbst
Von ferne zu, von einer höheren Warte aus und
Hochnäsig wie ein Mann auf einem Sprungbrett,
Der immer fort nur wippt, weil er nicht springen kann.

Und dann erschien sie im nebligen Hinterland,
Unsere Schlammvision, als ob sich eine Fensterrose
Aus Schlamm selbst aus der glitzernden Feuchte erfunden
Hätte, ein Hauchgespinst kreiste zentriert um die eigene
Nabe aus verschwommenem Schmutz, besudelt, doch leuchtend.
Von der Sonne, die stillstand, der Sonne,
Die sich verfärbte, wußten wir schon, doch uns wurde
Richtige Erde zuteil, verklärt und im Wirbel.
Dann ging die Sonne trüb unter, gelang es
Dem Wischer nie ganz, die Scheibe zu säubern,
Schmeckten Zisternen nach Schlick, sammelte sich
In den Haaren und Brauen ein leichtes Geflock,
Begann mancher, einen Klecks auf der Stirne zu tragen,
Um gegen alles gewappnet zu sein. Vigilien
An matschigen Spalten kamen in Schwang,
Auf Altären wichen die Lilien dem Schilf,
Und Invaliden bevölkerten im Turnus
Bettstätten zur Miete in Reichweite des Schauers.

A generation who had seen a sign!
Those nights when we stood in an umber dew and smelled
Mould in the verbena, or woke to a light
Furrow-breath on the pillow, when the talk
Was all about who had seen it and our fear
Was touched with a secret pride, only ourselves
Could be adequate then to our lives. When the rainbow
Curved flood-brown and ran like a water-rat's back
So that drivers on the hard shoulder switched off to watch,
We wished it away, and yet we presumed it a test
That would prove us beyond expectation.

We lived, of course, to learn the folly of that.
One day it was gone and the east gable
Where its trembling corolla had balanced
Was starkly a ruin again, with dandelions
Blowing high up on the ledges, and moss
That slumbered on through its increase. As cameras raked
The site from every angle, experts
Began their *post factum* jabber and all of us
Crowded in tight for the big explanations.
Just like that, we forgot that the vision was ours,
Our one chance to know the incomparable
And dive to a future. What might have been origin
We dissipated in news. The clarified place
Had retrieved neither us nor itself – except
You could say we survived. So say that, and watch us
Who had our chance to be mud-men, convinced and estranged,
Figure in our own eyes for the eyes of the world.

Ein Geschlecht hatte ein Zeichen gesehen!
Diese Nächte, da wir im Umbra-Tau standen und Schimmel
Im Eisenkraut rochen oder von einem leichten
Furchenhauch auf dem Kissen erwachten, als es immer
Nur darum ging, wer es gesehen hatte, und unsere Angst
Eine Spitze von heimlichem Stolz barg: da konnten nur wir
Unsrem Leben genügen. Als der Regenbogen sich flutbraun
Wölbte und wie der Rücken einer Wasserratte troff,
Daß Fahrer auf dem Seitenstreifen hielten, um zu schauen,
Wünschten wir sie fort und sahen sie doch als Prüfung,
Die wir – jenseits aller Erwartung – bewältigen würden.

Natürlich ging der Irrsinn uns noch auf.
Eines Tags war sie fort, und der Ostgiebel,
Wo ihr zitternder Blütenkranz geschwebt hatte,
War platterdings wieder Ruine, Löwenzahnsamen
Wehten empor auf Gesimse, und Moose
Hatten ihr Wachstum verschlummert. Kameras durchpflügten
Die Stätte aus jedem Winkel, das Post-festum-
Gequassel der Experten hub an, und wir alle
Drängten uns vor nach den Großen Erklärungen.
Einfach so – uns entfiel, daß es *unsre* Vision war,
Unsere eine Chance, das Unvergleichliche zu schauen
Und ein Morgen zu finden. Ein möglicher Ursprung
Wurde zernachrichtet. Geklärt hatte der Ort
Weder uns noch sich selbst wiederhergestellt – außer
Du sagtest, wir überlebten. So sag es, und sieh uns,
Die wir unsere Chance vertaten, Schlamm-Menschen zu sein,
Überzeugt und entfremdet, Zeichen in unseren Augen
Für die Augen der Welt.

The Disappearing Island

Once we presumed to found ourselves for good
Between its blue hills and those sandless shores
Where we spent our desperate night in prayer and vigil,

Once we had gathered driftwood, made a hearth
And hung our cauldron like a firmament,
The island broke beneath us like a wave.

The land sustaining us seemed to hold firm
Only when we embraced it *in extremis*.
All I believe that happened there was vision.

Die verschwindende Insel

Kaum wagten wir, endgültig Fuß zu fassen
Zwischen ihren blauen Hügeln und dem Uferland,
Wo wir verzweifelt unsre Nacht durchwachten,

Kaum hatten wir Treibholz gesammelt, Feuer gemacht
Und unsern Kessel aufgehängt wie eine Feste,
Zerschellte uns die Insel wie eine Woge.

Die Erde, die uns trug, schien erst zu halten,
Als wir sie *in extremis* an uns drückten.
Alles, was ich geschehen sah, war Vision.

The Riddle

You never saw it used but still can hear
The sift and fall of stuff hopped on the mesh,

Clods and buds in a little dust-up,
The dribbled pile accruing under it.

Which would be better, what sticks or what falls through?
Or does the choice itself create the value?

Legs apart, deft-handed, start a mime
To sift the sense of things from what's imagined

And work out what was happening in that story
Of the man who carried water in a riddle.

Was it culpable ignorance, or was it rather
A *via negativa* through drops and let-downs?

Gerätsel

Nie sahst du ihn in Gebrauch, doch hörst du noch,
Wie es auf dem Gitter hüpft, dann rieselt, fällt,

Klumpen und Knospen etwas Staub aufwirbeln,
Das Durchgesiebte sich darunter häuft.

Was ist nun besser, was bleibt oder was durchfällt?
Oder entsteht der Wert erst durch die Auswahl?

Mime nun, breitbeinig und behende,
Die Scheidung der Bedeutung vom Gedachten

Und find heraus, was die Geschichte meinte –
Vom Mann, der Wasser in einem Durchwurf trug.

War es sträfliche Ignoranz, oder wars eher
Eine *via negativa* durch Frust und Versieben?

Inhalt

Alphabets 8
Alphabete 9
Terminus 10
Grenzstation 11
From the Frontier of Writing 18
Von der Grenze des Schreibens 19
The Haw Lantern 20
Die Hagebuttenlaterne 21
The Stone Grinder 22
Der Steinschleifer 23
A Daylight Art 24
Eine Tageslicht-Kunst 25
Parable Island 26
Parabolische Insel 27
From the Republic of Conscience 30
Aus der Republik des Gewissens 31
Hailstones 34
Hagelkörner 35
Two Quick Notes 38
Zwei Briefchen 39
The Stone Verdict 40
Das Stein-Verdikt 41
From the Land of the Unspoken 42
Aus dem Land des Unausgesprochenen 43
A Ship of Death 46
Ein Schiff des Todes 47
The Spoonbait 48
Der Blinker 49
In Memoriam: Robert Fitzgerald 50
In memoriam Robert Fitzgerald 51
The Old Team 52
Die alte Mannschaft 53
Clearances 54
Lichtungen 55

The Milk Factory	72
Die Milchfabrik	73
The Summer of Lost Rachel	74
Der Sommer der verlorenen Rahel	75
The Wishing Tree	78
Der Wunschbaum	79
A Postcard from Iceland	80
Eine Postkarte aus Island	81
A Peacock's Feather	82
Eine Pfauenfeder	83
Grotus and Coventina	86
Grotus und Coventina	87
Holding Course	88
Auf Kurs bleiben	89
The Song of the Bullets	90
Das Lied der Geschosse	91
Wolfe Tone	94
Wolfe Tone	95
A Shooting Script	96
Ein Exposé	97
From the Canton of Expectation	98
Aus dem Kanton der Erwartung	99
The Mud Vision	102
Die Schlammvision	103
The Disappearing Island	106
Die verschwindende Insel	107
The Riddle	108
Gerätsel	109

NOBELPREIS FÜR LITERATUR 1995

SEAMUS HEANEY

»Der irische Schriftsteller Seamus Heaney ist, wie Joyce, Yeats, Beckett und andere vor ihm, eine literarische Stimme für die Welt.« DIE ZEIT

Seamus Heaney
Die Hagebuttenlaterne
GEDICHTE

112 Seiten. Aus dem Englischen von Giovanni Bandini und Ditte König

Seamus Heaney
Ausgewählte Gedichte

160 Seiten. Aus dem Englischen von Giovanni Bandini und Ditte König

Seamus Heaney
Die Herrschaft der Sprache
ESSAYS UND VORLESUNGEN

224 Seiten. Aus dem Englischen und mit einem Nachwort von Alexander Schmitz